Love – Luck – Trust

love letters to my child

love letters to you,

love letters to my child

Editor
The Brilliant Company

Bibliographic information of the German National Library:
The German National Library lists this publication in the Deutsche Natio-
nalbibliografie; detailed bibliographic data are available on the Internet via
dnb.dnb.de.

Production and publishing: BoD - Books on Demand, Norderstedt

ISBN 9-783-752-628-708

Loreen Ialazzo
www.thebrilliantbook.de
www.thebrilliantmom.de

love letters to my child

My beloved child

To you I write these letters, because I am full of love and I would like to give you something precious, one day. You mean so much to me and give me my strength, perseverance and inspiration for life.

You are my World.

I want to thank you from the bottom of my heart for being here, for being who you are and for choosing me as your mom.

With this book I would like to show you a piece of my world with hope that you will forever know how much I love you.

In my letters to you, I try to preserve important moments between the two of us: fantastic, funny, exciting, maybe critical, but always valuable experiences so you can always remember them. I would like to tell you honestly about my fears, my hopes and, of course, some well-intentioned and seriously tested advice.

I take my time to write my love letters to you and even paint, scribble or rhyme. In any case, I will be creative – for you.

You are my pride. You challenge me to be a better self and you show me what's really important: Love, contentedness and trust.

You can count on me. Allways. I am there for you.

I love you.

Date

I love you

Darling

you are wonderfull

I am your Mother
You are my Child.
I am your quiet place
You are my wild.
I am your calm face
You are my giggle.
I am your wait
You are my wiggle.
I am your dinner
You are my chocolate cake.
I am your bedtime
You are my wide awake.
I am your lullaby
You are my peek-a-boo.
I am your good night kiss
You are my I love You.

Date

Had I not created
My whole World,
I would certainly have died
in other people´s.

- Anaïs Nin

Happiness
is an inside job

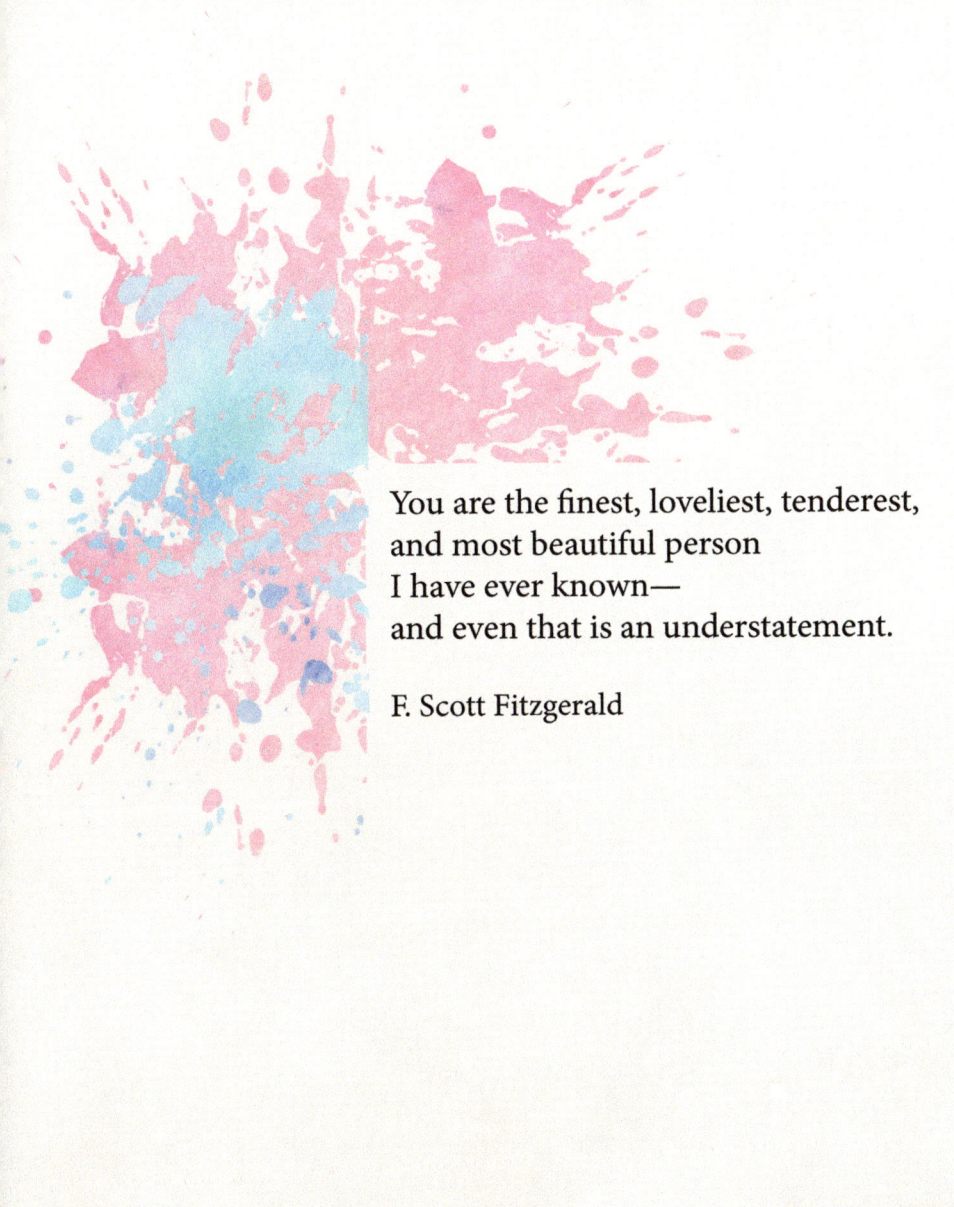

You are the finest, loveliest, tenderest,
and most beautiful person
I have ever known—
and even that is an understatement.

F. Scott Fitzgerald

Date

and at the end of the day
your feet should be dirty.
your hair messy and
your eyes sparkling.

shanti

Be free

April fool

It is more *important.*
to give your best than
to be the best.

- Mom & Dad.

Weak people, revenge.

Strong people, forgive.

Smart people, ignore

ein Albert Einstein Albert Einstein Albert Einstein Alb

Little Sunshine

You make my day

The happy mom
has a happy child.
That's why I take care of
myself, my thoughts & actions.

And what really and always
at anytime makes me happy
is
YOU.

Date

It is better
to fail in *originality*

than to
succeed in imitation.

- Herman Melville

Date

Breathe in, breathe out

Life is beautiful

Live your life.
Eat with hands.
Shower with sand.
Wash yourself with mud.
Dance through the rain.
Smile at the people.
Appreciate the beauty of all cultures.
Learn from animals.
Use your senses.
Always be faithful.
Go through the world with an open heart.
I'm waiting for you with open arms,
when you want to come home.

I love you.